The Feelings Diary

Helping pupils to develop their emotional literacy skills by becoming more aware of their feelings on a daily basis.

by
Gillian Shotton

Suitable for use at key stages 2 and 3

ISBN 1 904315 00 3

Published by Lucky Duck Publishing Ltd
3 Thorndale Mews, Clifton, Bristol, BS8 2HX, UK

www.luckyduck.co.uk

Commissioned by George Robinson
Designed by Helen Weller
Printed by The Book Factory, London N1

Contents

"I write myself into well-being." Nancy Mair

"Whatever games are played with us, we must play no games with ourselves, but deal in our privacy with the last honesty and truth."
Ralph Waldo Emerson

"Lying to ourselves is more deeply ingrained than lying to others."
Fyodor Dostoyevski

"We honour ourselves and our friends when we tell them how we feel."
Theodore Isaac Rubin

Introduction

Emotional Literacy can be defined as the ability to recognise, understand and appropriately express your emotions. This is something that is very to difficult to do all of the time. We often find that we are not even aware of how we are feeling, yet those feelings have a powerful impact on our behaviour. For some of us, the problem is that we seldom express our feelings, keeping them securely pressed down inside. But sometimes they leak out when we don't want them to. For others, the problem is more about expressing those feelings appropriately, in the right time, place and manner, without making ourselves look ridiculous or letting others get hurt.

It's comforting to think that this is by no means a new problem, Aristotle also felt that emotional literacy was not an easy task. In talking about expressing anger he said,

"Anyone can become angry- that is easy. But to become angry with the right person, to the right degree, at the right time, for the right purpose, and in the right way – this is not easy." Aristotle, *The Nichomachean Ethics* (quoted in Goleman, 1995)

In his book *Nurturing Emotional Literacy* (2001) Peter Sharp explains that emotional literacy matters because:

▸ We need to recognise our emotions in order to label or define them

▸ We need to understand our emotions in order to be effective learners

▸ We need to handle (or manage) our emotions in order to develop positive and wholesome relationships

▸ We need to appropriately express our emotions in order to develop as rounded people capable of helping ourselves, and so become emotionally healthy. In turn, we will be better able to help others

We have all experienced being unable to concentrate or give our full attention to our work because of an argument with a close friend or difficulties at home, and so it is with children. Goleman (1995) writes how the physiology of the brain means that learning and strong emotions compete for space in working memory. Both negative and positive feelings have an influence on learning, memory and problem solving skills, as well as how we relate to others. Most teachers will have experienced the impact that negative feelings can have on the atmosphere in class and the subsequent levels of learning that result.

How can we help to develop childrens' emotional literacy?

One of the first steps to developing emotional literacy is getting in touch with your own feelings – actually realising what it is that you are feeling and why you might be feeling that way. Goleman writes that: "emotions that simmer beneath the threshold of awareness can have a powerful impact on how we perceive things and react, even though we have no idea that they are at work." A useful analogy is to think of our emotions as being the rudder of our boat, steering us in a particular direction, on a particular course of action. If we have little awareness of our feelings (which way the rudder is turned, what is going on under the water), then we may end up going in the wrong direction and finding ourselves where we do not want to be – maybe in the path of a steam liner! Emotional self-awareness is fundamental for managing our emotions. For example, becoming aware that I feel angry because someone belittled me in some way, gives me the power to choose to do something about it that will help me to change those feelings or shake off my bad mood.

One way to develop a higher degree of emotional awareness is to record your feelings in a diary. This also has the advantage that it gives you time to reflect on your feelings in private, working out what you feel and why. Many pupils do not feel comfortable or are unable to talk about their feelings without first having had the time to reflect. Writing feelings down in a diary is a useful interim step to being able to talk about them. Thinking and writing about what you are feeling and why you might be feeling that way, also has a cathartic effect and can help restore feelings of peace again.

The problem with giving a child a blank diary though, is that they often do not have, or are unable to access, the words they need to accurately describe how they are feeling. Other than 'happy' or 'sad' they don't know where to start. This is why I created the feelings diary. The diary has a page for each day of the week. Each page contains illustrations and words for a range of emotions we all experience from time to time. The illustrations are useful as they make the diary accessible even to those who are unable to read the words.

Does using the diary really do any good?

Research findings

The diary is used in a variety of groups that myself and other educational psychologists have run in schools. It has also been used extensively in interventions for individuals. The pupils who have been given the diary to use are generally individuals who have been identified as having difficulty with some aspect of emotional literacy. For example, they might have difficulty in expressing their anger appropriately, or in relating successfully with teachers and peers. The majority of groups have been at key stages two and three with a variety of foci, e.g. anger management, social skills, stress management, interpersonal communication, friendship skills and so on. The diary has also been used by teachers in an anger/stress management group I have run. Both pupils and teachers have commented that they have found the diary helpful and that they enjoyed using it. However, until the study described here, I had never actually carried out any formal research to discover if using the diary would make any measurable difference to their emotional awareness and ability to handle their feelings more effectively.

The participants in the study were 24 children in year five (nine to 10 year olds). With the help of a colleague, Adrian Faupel (Senior Educational Psychologist), a questionnaire was constructed to measure the pupils' levels of emotional awareness and their ability to express their emotions appropriately.

The questionnaire presented the children with a series of statements. They had to decide how true each of them was on a five point scale. Below is an example of one of the questions investigating emotional expression:

"If I feel really angry I take it out on someone in a nasty way, e.g. I shout at them or punch them."

Not true of me	Hardly ever true of me	Sometimes true of me	Often true of me	Very true of me

The children were told that there were no right or wrong answers and were they assured that no one would see their answers but me. So they could be really honest about where they felt they were at. With the help of the class teacher, the questionnaire was read to any children with literacy difficulties.

Having completed the questionnaire, I explained the feelings diary to the children. Many of them were very excited about using the diary and brainstormed where and when they might fill it in each day. Most of them said they would use it in their bedroom at bedtime. Some had ideas about filling it in under the bedclothes with a torch! The idea of having a special time and place where they could write things down just for them had great appeal.

During the week the class teacher conducted a couple of circle time sessions which focused on the pupils sharing feelings and events they had recorded in their diaries, to keep the task of daily recording fresh in their minds. As with all circle time sessions, the option to share or to pass was available. At the end of the week I returned and gave out certificates to those who had completed the diary consistently for the week. The questionnaire was then re-administered to see if there had been any change in the childrens' levels of emotional awareness and expression.

A little disappointingly, only half the class had remembered to fill in the diary consistently every day over the week. However, the results showed that for the children who consistently filled in the diary everyday, there was a significant increase in their combined level of emotional awareness and emotional expression. This shows that when used consistently, even just for one week, recording feelings using the feelings diary can help pupils to increase their emotional awareness as well as their ability to express their feelings more effectively.

I also asked the pupils to complete a separate, more qualitative questionnaire asking them what they thought they had got out of using the diary and what they liked about it. A few of the comments included:

- "I found it helpful as you could write down your feelings without anyone knowing."
- "It helped me control my feelings – you could write anything you wanted."
- "It helped me not to bottle up my feelings."
- "It was fun!"
- "It helped me to know and understand my feelings."

Guidance Notes

What age range is the diary suitable for?

The diary has been used successfully with pupils from key stage two and key stage three. As mentioned previously, it has also been used by adults, so there is definitely potential for using it at key stage four. Much will depend on the individual pupil(s) at key stage four. There is a possibility that some pupils might perceive the cartoon style of the diary as being patronising, whereas others would really like it. I have found that much depends on the 'leaders' within the group or class and their reaction to the diary. If they evaluate it as being credible, then the other pupils tend to follow suit. However, if one or two of the leaders voice that they think the diary is childish and beneath them, then again the others in the group tend to also hold the diary in less esteem and are less inclined to use it. Key stage one pupils in year two, who are quite able, might also be able to access the diary. Here again, the key is knowing the individual pupil(s) and perhaps even trying out the technique by photocopying one of the pages and using it with the pupil(s) in question, before going to the trouble of making up the diary as a whole. The cartoon style of the pictures does seem to be appreciated by most ages. Indeed, both myself and many of the teachers in the stress and anger management groups I have run have enjoyed using the diary and have found it a useful tool for helping you recognise and understand your feelings. It's not just pupils who need a little help in becoming more emotionally aware – we all do! If you haven't tried keeping a feelings diary yourself, then this would be a good time to start. In that way you will have a better idea of what is involved and what the benefits are, as well as being less critical of the pupils if they forget to fill it in sometimes, as you may have lapsed as well!

How to use the diary

The diary can be used with individual pupils, small groups, or as part of a whole class initiative on developing emotional literacy. The idea is that each day the pupil spends some time thinking about how they have felt during that day. They then circle the feeling (or most usually feelings) which best describes the emotions they have experienced during the day. A space at the bottom of each page allows them to write or draw why they think they might be feeling that way. At the back of the diary is a list of suggestions for helping them to change their feelings if they are not comfortable with them. Pupils need to know that the diary is private, so that they can feel free to record their feelings with honesty and without fear that someone else is going to look at what they have written.

Pupils will be more likely to develop the habit of recording their feelings if a special time in school (10 minutes at the end of the day for example) can be devoted to writing their diary. Otherwise, pupils tend to start the week with good intentions of writing their diary every day at home, but somehow the momentum disappears. It's fair to say that the same is true for all of us. Our good intentions of going to the gym everyday are more likely to succeed if we have a friend that makes us go with them. Like physical exercise, you know that filling in the diary (emotional exercise in a sense) will do you good, but it's hard to do it everyday when it's just you on your own and there's something good on the television! If the diaries are to be kept in school, care should be taken to store them in a secure place so that the pupils' privacy is maintained.

Using the diary with individuals

In my role as an educational psychologist I see many individual pupils who I suggest try using the feelings diary. These are pupils who need a little bit of extra input to help them develop an awareness of their feelings and express them appropriately. Often they are pupils who don't talk to their parents or friends about the uncomfortable feelings such as anger, guilt or loneliness that they have inside, so these feelings come out in other ways – physical/verbal aggression, using self harm, or being possessive with one particular friendship. Depending on the age and circumstances of the pupil, the diary can be used with individuals in a number of ways:

> The pupil shares the feelings they record on a daily basis with a trusted adult. This approach can be used to facilitate daily communication between a pupil and parent or between a pupil and a trusted adult in school (for example a support assistant or teacher, with whom the pupil has built up a strong relationship).

Case study

Joely, an eight year old girl, was extremely shy, sensitive and lacking in confidence. Sometimes she was teased by the other girls in her class which made her feel even more worthless. She just didn't know how to respond. Joely kept her feelings inside, she never talked to anyone about what she was going through. Her mum and dad were loving parents but they were not people who talked about their feelings particularly, so Joely didn't have a model of how she might do this. She thought her feelings and difficulties were all her own to sort out and she didn't think anyone else would be interested. She also didn't want to be a burden to anyone as she was afraid that then they might not like her. Joely became more and more withdrawn in school and started to pull her hair out of her head, strand by strand. She would also cut her arm using a compass. Her parents and teacher became extremely concerned. Joely used the feelings diary in close conjunction with her mother, who desperately wanted Joely to talk to her but couldn't find a way in. The diary proved to be that way in. Each evening Joely would fill in the diary and then talk about her feelings with her mum. Through this regular special time Joely felt much better. She began to realise that her feelings were important and that she didn't have to work all her difficulties out by herself. By talking through the incidents that occurred with the

---

group of girls in school, her mum was able to help her think of alternative ways she could respond to the girls, and when she should tell her teacher. Over time, Joely grew in confidence and was able to not only talk to her mum about her feelings but also her teacher and one of her friends. The self harming behaviour stopped and Joely started to answer questions in class. She even gave a talk to her class about her interest in horses.

This approach can only be used where both the adult and pupil feel comfortable sharing together on this level. In the case study, Joely welcomed using the diary and sharing what she wrote with her mum. Other pupils, particularly older pupils, might balk at the idea of sharing their intimate feelings with their mum or an adult in school. The key is always to check out with the pupil what they would find helpful.

The pupil uses the diary, either at home or at school, and has an individual session once a week with a trusted adult in school, where they can choose to share something from their diary.

In this way, the diary is much more of a private exercise for the pupil, but they are still supported in using it. It is not left up to them to get on with using it totally on their own. Using the diary in this way gives the message that the pupil's feelings are important and worth hearing about. The diary can be a useful vehicle for communication between a pupil and the trusted adult in school.

Case Study

John, a year eight pupil, had difficulty in managing his anger. He was always getting into trouble for flying off the handle at teachers or peers, either at break times or in lessons. John really wanted to be able to control his anger better, as he didn't like getting detentions and temporary exclusions. He also felt terrible following an angry outburst. However, once he was in a certain situation, he would find himself being taken over by the angry feelings again. John was given a feelings diary to use over a six week period. He was given 10 minutes at the end of each day where he could go to the Head of Years office and spend time writing down how he had felt that day and why. He then had a weekly session with his Head of Year (with whom he had a good relationship). In this session he spoke about the times during the week when he had felt angry: the reasons why he had felt angry; and how he had been able to calm down again. Over a few weeks, simply recording and talking about how he dealt with his angry feelings helped John to realise the most potent triggers for his anger. It also helped him to realise what he could do and think about both at the time and afterwards in order to manage his angry feelings. The number of incidents of angry outbursts consequently decreased as John was able to develop an action plan of what he would do and say in common problem situations in order to manage his anger more effectively.

The weekly individual session could focus on the management of one particular emotion, as with John managing his angry feelings, or each session could look at a different emotion. The approach of looking at a different emotion each week helps the pupil to develop an overall awareness of their feelings, and helps them to become aware of how they tend to react when they have particular feelings. For example, Lauren, a year seven pupil, became aware that whenever she had anxious feelings she would start to eat. She was using food as a way of trying to suppress her anxious feelings, as she didn't know how to deal with these feelings. Developing her awareness that she was using this coping strategy helped Lauren find other things she could do to comfort herself when she felt anxious. Many of the activities described in the six week programme of work (later outlined) could easily be adapted for use with an individual. For example, the table of suggested strategies for helping pupils manage their anger could easily be discussed with a pupil on an individual basis rather than within a whole class or small group setting. Similarly, the circle time sentence completion rounds could also be used on an individual basis as conversation starters, with both the pupil and the trusted adult sharing on "something that helps me to relax is…" or whatever the sentence completion round is for that week.

Using the diary with small groups

There may be a group of pupils in your class or year group who you feel would particularly benefit from using the diary in a weekly session that would reinforce and complement its use. There are many advantages of carrying out this work in small group setting (usually with six to eight pupils and an adult facilitator) rather than in a whole class.

▶ The pupils find support from one another as they get to know one another better in the small group

▶ It is much easier to build a climate of trust within a small group

▶ Quieter group members can develop the confidence to speak in front of their peers

▶ Pupils feel safe enough to share on a more intimate and real level

▶ For many pupils, such groups become a fundamental support mechanism that they haven't received anywhere else – helping to build their self-esteem and confidence

The disadvantage in terms of using the feelings diary in the small group setting is that it is often difficult to find time for the pupils to fill in their diaries in school each day if the rest of their class are not doing it as well. It may be possible for arrangements to be made for one or two pupils to have 10 minutes in a private place at the end of the school day to write their diaries (as described in John's case study), but organising for a whole group to leave the class at the end of the day can be awkward and might also result in the pupils feeling singled out, as their group exit would be quite obvious. If the diary cannot be filled out in school, then it is up to the pupil to fill it out at home. If this is to be the case, time at the first session should be spent brainstorming with the pupils where and when they are going to fill it in, where they are going to keep it, and how they are going to remind themselves to fill it in, for example a 'post-it' on the bedroom mirror. Asking parents to give their son or daughter a gentle reminder to fill it in each evening is also a good idea.

The activities described in the six week programme of work could easily be adapted for use in a small group. The group would meet for approximately 45 minutes on a weekly basis. The group is ideally led by two adults, one to lead and the other to observe. It is useful to start each session off by outlining the rules of the group.

Group Rules

▶ Listen when someone is speaking – don't interrupt

▶ Only say positive things about other members of the group – no put downs or dirty looks

▶ If you don't want to say something, then you may pass

▶ Don't repeat things you have heard in the group when you're outside the group

---

The pupils should be informed that they will be asked to bring their diaries to the group each week. This isn't so that others can read what they've written, but for them to refer to. They may be asked to share something from that week's entries (optional, no pressure if they don't want to) or they may be given the opportunity to look back over their entries to identify patterns of feelings over time, (for example "I always feel worried on a Tuesday because I have to sit next to Martin in science and he keeps talking to me!").

The circle time approach, where an object is passed round to identify whose turn it is to speak, can also be a useful tool in a small group setting with six to eight pupils, especially if they have particular difficulties with turn taking and listening. More informal discussion and sharing can take place in a smaller group without the need for an object to identify who is speaking.

Having drinks and biscuits at the end of the group cannot be underestimated in terms of its importance. It gives the pupils time to talk to one another and gives an added incentive for attendance. A year eight boy in one of the groups I led was allergic to orange squash, so a different drink was provided for him each week. This small act seemed to have a profound effect on his perception of the group. He looked forward to coming each week and was a more willing participant. He said that no-one had done that for him within school before.

Using the diary with a whole class

Using the diary with a whole class means that everyone gets to try out using it and discover if it's a strategy that will help them. This is positive because within any group of children or adults, you will find those for whom writing is a useful tool and others who find that writing down their feelings isn't so helpful. However, it's only through trying out a variety of strategies that you find what works best for you, so giving your class or tutor group the opportunity to try using the diary is a really positive step. Perhaps you will be introducing them to a strategy that will help them throughout their lives.

Introducing the diary

Before giving out the diaries it is important to spend some time discussing with the class the importance of recognising your emotions and being able to express them appropriately. Ask them to relate times when perhaps they didn't express their feelings appropriately, such as times when they felt really angry and took their anger out on someone who wasn't really to blame. Road rage is a useful example of people being unable to handle and appropriately express their feelings. Keep the conversation non-judgmental, after all, we've all had times when we haven't handled our feelings very well. As well as the 'acting out' types of examples, it is useful to talk about individuals who don't express their feelings at all, but just keep them bottled up inside. A good example might be a pupil who gets bullied at school but never tells anyone or expresses their anxiety. Their anxieties get worse and worse until eventually they refuse to come to school – they can't face it anymore. Ask the pupils if anyone has experienced anything like this, where they just kept their feelings locked up inside and didn't tell anyone what was going on. Perhaps they didn't even acknowledge to themselves how they felt.

Talk about how it is not good for us to keep feelings locked up inside. It affects our health as well as the way that we get one with other people. A good analogy to use here is that of a sponge getting full of water. Just like a sponge, when we become full of negative feelings they may start to leak out inadvertently. We need to find a way of releasing the feelings bit by bit, when we want to let them out, rather than them coming out in inappropriate ways when we don't want them to. One useful way of understanding and expressing your feelings is to write them down in a diary.

Ask if anyone has used a diary before and if they found it helpful. Show them one of the diaries and explain how to fill it in. Explain that they fill it in at the end of the day as they reflect on the main emotions they have had during that day. They may of course circle a number of emotions for each day (it usually will be more than one) then underneath they write a brief note as to why they felt that way.

Discuss with them where and when they're going to fill the diary in. If it is to be in school, then it is most useful to have some time at the end of the school day. If the pupils are going to take the diaries home, then you need to discuss with them when and where they are going to fill it in.

Ask them to bring the diary along to the session each week. Explain that they will not be expected to show what they have written, but they may be asked to look back in their diaries to remind themselves. If the diaries are going to be kept in school, the pupils need to feel that they will be kept in a place where no one has access to them, so their privacy is maintained.

Privacy and child protection issues

Usually the contents of the diary remain private unless a pupil decides to share them. However, there are situations where the diary might be used in a more overt way, usually with younger children on an individual basis (see Joely case study). The key here is to ask the pupil in what way they would feel comfortable using the diary and if they would feel comfortable sharing what they have written. Pupils should be informed that what they share will remain confidential unless it is something where they may be in a dangerous situation, in which case confidentiality cannot be maintained.

How long should the diary be kept for?

It is really it's up to you. The diary can be made up to cover just one week to try it out, or for anything up to a term's worth of weeks. Just photocopy the necessary number of weeks and slot them into the booklets accordingly. The programme of work outlined is made up to cover six weeks (approximately half a term) which would give a reasonable amount of time for the pupils to use the diary and for a variety of extension activities to be organised that complement its use, helping to improve emotional literacy even further.

A six week programme of activities to support the use of the diary

These activities are designed in to complement the use of the feelings diary, helping pupils take their emotional awareness further and begin to develop some useful strategies for dealing with uncomfortable feelings such as anger or fear.

Circle time is a useful format for many of the discussions and activities to take place. If you are unfamiliar with the circle time approach, I suggest you read *Circle Time, an activity book for teachers* by Teresa Bliss and Jo Tetley (1993) in order to gain an understanding of how it is carried out in class. The pupils and teacher sit in a circle, either on chairs or cushions on the floor, but the important thing is that everyone can be seen by everyone else. When the talking object, for example a stone or shell, is passed round the circle, only the person who is holding it may speak. The rules for circle time should be outlined on each occasion. After a few times it is a good idea to ask the pupils to state the rules at the beginning of each session rather than the teacher reading them out.

Circle time rules

▸ We listen when someone else is speaking

▸ We may pass if we don't want to say anything

▸ Keep it positive (no put downs or dirty looks)

This programme is designed for use with a whole class but could easily be adapted for use with a small group. Many of the activities are also suitable for use with individuals. Around 40 to 50 minutes should be allowed for each session. Alternatively, the session could be split into two 20 minute sessions, holding the circle time rounds and discussions in the first session and carrying out the other activities in the second session. This would enable the programme to fit more easily into tutor time for secondary schools.

Week 1: **Anger**

Circle time sentence completion round (using their diaries to help them look up the sorts of things that have made them angry over the past week):

▶ "I feel angry when…"

Discussion

What helps you calm down when you feel angry? Brainstorm their ideas under two headings:
A) things they can think, say or do at the time to stop them reacting in a way they might regret later and
B) things they can do later on to help them calm down and feel peaceful again.

Leave the sheet of ideas up as reminders during the week.

A few ideas to get you going…

When you feel like you are about to explode	Later on, or when you get the chance
Things to say to yourself: ▶ 'I feel angry but I don't have to react.' ▶ 'I can ignore them.' ▶ 'This feeling will pass.' *Things to do:* ▶ Ignore them, walk away or ask to sit somewhere else ▶ Think of a special place ▶ Focus on relaxing your muscles ▶ Count to 30 ▶ Imagine a shield or a tortoise shell all around you – nothing can get in, you are safe	▶ Have some quiet time on your own ▶ Talk about what happened with someone you can trust ▶ Take some exercise, go for a walk or play footy ▶ Write down how you are feeling and why in your diary ▶ Do something you know you will enjoy – go and see a friend or watch a programme on TV that makes you laugh, listen to your favourite music, or read a book

Activity

Draw a picture to show what your anger looks like (e.g. a volcano).

Or

Make a card to keep in your pocket for times when you are feeling angry. Write on the card three different strategies that you think will work for you when you feel angry.

Homework

Ask them to notice, particularly over the coming week, things that help them to calm down after they have felt angry. Challenge them to try out one of the strategies that came up during the discussion.

For next week ask them to bring in a photo of a place where they felt very relaxed, perhaps somewhere they went to on holiday.

For further information on anger and managing it effectively, you might like to read *Anger Management, A Practical Guide* by Faupel, Herrick and Sharp (1998).

Managing Anger, Stories and Activities based on Punch and the Pawn by Angwin and Foster (2001) Primary Age

Crucial Skills, An Anger Management and Problem Solving Teaching Programme for High School Students by Johnson and Rae (1999) Secondary Age.

Keep your Coooool Stress Reducing Strategies for Key Stages 2 & 3 by Rae and Robinson (2001).

Week 2 : **Peaceful / Calm / Relaxed**

Circle time sentence completion round (using their diaries to remind them):

▸ "Something that helps me relax is when I…"

Discussion

Did anyone feel angry over the last week? If so, did they use one of the strategies discussed? Ask them to share what it was and how effective it was for helping them feel calm again. If the pupils are not able to share an example, then you need to share one, so remember to have one up your sleeve! Sometimes this is all that's needed to open up discussion.

Individual activity

Ask those pupils who have remembered to bring in a photo of a relaxing place (part of their homework last week) to talk about the photo. Ask them to talk about where the place was geographically, and what it was about the place that made them feel relaxed. Pupils who have not remembered to bring a photo can draw a picture of a place where they felt peaceful, relaxed and happy. Make a class display of relaxing places. Talk with the pupils about how, even though you can't be physically transported to your favourite place when you are feeling upset or angry, you can close your eyes and go there in your head. For some pupils it may be useful to carry a small picture of their favourite place in their pocket as a reminder, to help them imagine that they're there when they need to relax.

Whole class relaxation exercise (10 minutes)

For pupils to become more aware of the physical difference between tension and relaxation, it is useful to have a relaxation session. This is most effectively carried out in a room where the pupils are able to lie down in their own space, away from others who might distract them. If space is not sufficient for this then the relaxation can be carried out with them seated at their tables, but this method is not as effective. It helps to listen to a piece of ambient music. I find that Moby's album *Play* has some very calming tracks on it, but there are plenty of other 'chill out' CDs currently available. This type of ambient music makes relaxation more likely to be a success with older pupils.

The following can be read whilst the music is playing. It must be read quite slowly, pausing for a few seconds at appropriate points.

… I want you now to concentrate on the sound of my voice.

… Leave all other outside sounds behind.

… Concentrate on what I am saying and concentrate on relaxing.

… Starting at your head and working down to your feet, you are going to spot any parts of your body where you feel tight and tense, and slowly you are going to let that tension slip away.

… First of all, think about your forehead. Is it relaxed? No frowning, no lines, just a nice smooth forehead.

… Your eyes should be gently closed, your eyelashes just touching. Not screwed up or tight.

… Your mouth should be gently closed and your whole face should be quite expressionless and completely relaxed.

… Take a deep breath in (pause as you also take a breath in) and then let it go. Take another breath in (pause) then let it go. Think about your shoulders, are they relaxed?
Take a deep breath in and as you let it go feel your shoulders relax and drop down. Let them go all floppy and heavy.

… Now feel the weight of your arms. Feel your arms getting heavier and heavier. Relax your fingers. Your fingers should be gently open rather than tight fists.

… Now you are going to imagine that you have been magically transported to your special place. You are no longer here in this room, you are in your special place. Your safe place.

… Think about what it looks like. Is the sun shining?

… Is it warm or is it cool?

… What can you see all around you? Are there other people around?

… What do you imagine yourself doing? In your mind, take a little walk around and explore your special place.

… Now you've had the chance to explore it a little you're going to imagine yourself sitting down in it and resting.

… You feel completely at ease and relaxed. You are breathing very slowly now and very gently.

… In a moment you are going to leave your special place and get ready to be back in the room with me. Don't worry though, you can always go back there in your imagination any time you feel you need to. Perhaps when you're feeling upset or angry or very sad you can go back there. Counting back from five, leaving your place behind now.

… Four, become aware of the noises in the room.

> ... Three, open your eyes.
>
> ... Two, look around the room.
>
> ... One, slowly get up and walk around the room.

Gather the pupils back together and use the following questions to end the session with a useful discussion before giving out the homework.

- ▸ Where was your special place?
- ▸ What did you imagine yourself doing?
- ▸ Do you feel relaxed now?
- ▸ How does your body feel?
- ▸ Is this something you would like to do again?

Homework

Try to notice times over the coming week when you feel relaxed. Does it tend to be when you are in a particular place or when you are with particular people?

For next week ask them to bring in a piece of music (either on CD or tape) that makes them feel really happy when they listen to it.

Week 3: **Happy**

Circle time sentence completion round (using their diaries to remind them):

▶ "I feel happy when…"

Sharing music

Play excerpts of each person's music to the rest of the class (as with all circle time activities make it clear that no put downs or negative comments are allowed). Ask the person who has brought in the music to explain why they like it.

Individual activity

Looking back through their diary entries ask the pupils to count up the number of times they have circled that they have felt happy over the last few weeks. Using the photocopiable sheet 'Things that make me feel happy', get them to write or draw the things that have made them feel happy over the past two to three weeks. If they haven't had any 'happy' entries (perhaps they've been going through a rough time recently) ask them to think about a time when they did feel happy and write or draw about that on their sheet.

Homework

Take their sheet home and talk about the things they have written or drawn with their parents/carers. Ask the pupils to discuss with their parents/carers if there is anything they could do at home to help their parents/carers feel happy. Write or draw this in the box at the bottom of the sheet.

Things that make me feel happy

Something I can do to help someone at home feel happy…

Week 4: **Lonely**

To introduce the concept of loneliness and generate a fuller understanding, the following story can be read.

Hannah's family had just moved into the neighbourhood and Hannah would be going to the local school. It was half-way through the term and because of the move Hannah had had a few days off school. It felt weird to be out of school when she knew all her friends back in her old school were having lessons and getting on with stuff as normal. Hannah's best friend Susan had given her a card and a necklace as a leaving present. "Really going to miss you'" she had said. They were going to keep in touch with email and by using the phone, but it wasn't the same.

"First day at your new school tomorrow," her mum said.

Hannah sighed. She felt really anxious because she found it difficult at the best of times to talk to people, let alone people she had never met before.

"It'll be OK," said her mum reassuringly.

"Yeah I know," said Hannah, but she still felt really anxious.

The following day she was shown into her new classroom by the Head teacher. Hannah was given a seat on a table with three other girls – Lauren, Marie and Lorna. They were really nice and friendly towards her, but Hannah found it really difficult to talk to them. They didn't know her like her old friend Susan did. She could really talk to Susan and they used to have a really good laugh together. The conversation here felt awkward and uncomfortable. At break time Hannah stood at the edge of the playground area and watched the other pupils involved in their various games or just walking round in pairs or groups. She felt really lonely. Everyone else seemed to be really busy with their friends. They didn't seem to even notice she was there. She felt like she was invisible. She thought about Susan. If only she were here, she thought. She felt a bit embarrassed as well. Surely it was obvious to everyone that she was the new girl and she hadn't any friends, that she was just standing there on her own. That was the last thing she wanted, people to think she was really sad, someone who others didn't want to be friends with. "I know," she thought, "I'll act like it's all OK and walk round the playground. I'll make it look like I'm going to meet someone and I'll smile so they won't think I'm friendless and lonely, like I really am."

Discussion

- Have you ever felt lonely like this? And if so, when?
- Why did Hannah try to smile and act like she wasn't really feeling lonely?
- Have you ever tried to hide your feelings? Do you think it's a good strategy?
- What do you think Hannah could do in this situation? What helps you when you are feeling lonely?

Drama Activity

In small groups act out the story but make up an ending that helps Hannah start to feel less lonely. Each group could show their play to the rest of the class.

Homework

This week ask the pupils to keep a look out for people at break or lunchtime who are on their own. Go up to them and start a conversation, asking them to join you and your friends. It could make a big difference to how they're feeling.

Week 5: **Thankful**

Introducing the feeling

In his book *Don't Sweat The Small Stuff*, Richard Carlson 1997 describes how gratitude and inner peace go hand in hand. Focusing on the things in your life that you are genuinely grateful for is an effective way to take your mind off the negative thoughts, the fears, worries and complaints that so easily overtake us. The following story can help pupils see how this might work in practice

Sam lay awake and looked at the ceiling. Over in the corner his brother Thomas was sleeping soundly. He could see the duvet rise and gently fall with Thomas' breathing. Sam sighed deeply. It was no good, he couldn't get to sleep. His mind wouldn't shut down. He was thinking about his maths exam in school the next day. He had tried to revise but really he knew he hadn't done as much as he should have done. There was loads of stuff that might come up that he hadn't got a clue about. He kept thinking about all the questions that he might get, where he would be really stuck, and the thought of just sitting there not being able to do it just terrified him. The worst thing was, he knew that if he didn't get to sleep he would be in an even worse state the next day. He would feel so tired that even if questions did come up that he knew, he wouldn't be able to concentrate. "I've got to get to sleep!"He said aloud and punched his pillow hard to make it more comfy again. But how do you get to sleep when your mind won't shut down? Then Sam remembered his teacher talking about something she did when she felt worried – start listing all the things in her life she was really thankful for. "Well, it's worth a try," Sam thought, "even if I don't get to sleep, at least I won't feel as anxious as I do now." So Sam started to think.

Firstly, there was his mum and dad. They didn't live together anymore, but Sam was still really grateful for them both, because they both loved him and showed it in different ways. Dad took him out fishing and mum, well mum did loads of stuff for him – washing, cooking, making sure he had everything he needed, helping him with his homework. Sam was really grateful for all of this. Then there were his best friends – Eddie and Joe. They had such a good laugh together at school. Sam was really grateful for this too. Life would be pretty boring without Eddie and Joe around. He thought about the time in science when they just couldn't stop laughing because their teacher went cross-eyed every time he focused on the thermometer he was demonstrating with. Yeah, he was grateful for that as well, being able to have a laugh with his mates. Then there was his dog Scamp. He was a bit of a rascal but it was great having a dog because even when you were feeling really down, Scamp would come and lick your face and cheer you up a bit. As Sam carried on, he found he could think of loads of things he was thankful for, and thinking about them stopped him thinking about the test. It didn't seem half so important now that he really thought about it. By focusing on all the good stuff in his life, he had got things into perspective, and it wasn't long before he fell asleep.

Discussion

Brainstorm some of the things that you feel thankful for. Do you think that using the strategy of thinking of these things would help you at times when you are experiencing uncomfortable feelings?

Circle time sentence completion round (using their diaries to remind them):

▶ "This week I felt thankful for…"

Activity

Using the photocopiable thankful list, the pupils can identify five things they are thankful for today, illustrating the sheet if they want.

Homework

Over the following week, start each day thinking of three things you are thankful for, just whilst you are eating your breakfast or on the way to school. If it helps, you might like to list them in your diary. It doesn't matter if they are the same things on different days. The important thing is that you spent the time thinking about them and that you write them down.

Things I am thankful for

1

2

3

4

5

Week 6: **Worried / anxious**
(feeling uneasy, being troubled by something)

Brainstorm with the class things that often make people feel worried. Here are a few ideas to get you going:

- Starting a new school
- Changing school
- Parents arguing
- Being bullied
- Making decisions
- Moving house
- Homework
- Exams/tests
- Friends (arguments etc.)

Circle time sentence completion round:

- "Something that helps me when I feel worried is to…."

Again, here are a few ideas to get you going:

- Write your worries down on a piece of paper and put it in a box.
  Then, when the worry comes back into your mind, say to yourself, "I'm not allowing myself to think about this anymore. It's in the box and I've shut the lid!"
- Talk about how you are feeling with someone you can trust
- Put on some favourite music and dance around the room
- Go to see a friend
- Take some exercise
- Read a book that you really get into, for example Harry Potter

Activity

Ask the pupils to look back through their diaries and focus on the times when they have circled feeling worried. Using the photocopiable sheet 'Things that make me feel worried' ask the pupils to write or draw three things that have made them feel worried and list things they can do to help them stop worrying. Talk through what they have written or drawn with a partner.

Circle time discussion

▶ How have you found using the feelings diary? Was it helpful? Was it fun?

▶ Is it something you would like to continue using?

Things that make me feel worried

Things I can do when I feel this way:

1

2

3

References and useful resources

Angwin, F. and Foster, J. (2001) *Managing Anger*, Lucky Duck Publishing, Bristol.

Ban Breathnach, S. (1996) *Simple Abundance*, Bantam Books, London.

Bliss, T. and Tetley, J. (1993) *Circle Time, an activity book for teachers*, Lucky Duck Publishing, Bristol.

Carlson, R. (1997) *Don't Sweat The Small Stuff*, Hodder and Stoughton, London.

Faupel, A., Herrick, E., and Sharp, P. (1998) *Anger Management, A Practical Guide*, David Fulton, London.

Goleman, D. (1995) *Emotional Intelligence*, Bloomsbury, London.

Johnson, P. and Rae, T. (1999) *Crucial Skills*, Lucky Duck Publishing Ltd, Bristol.

Mosely, J. (1993) *Turn Your School Round*, LDA, Cambs.

Sharp, P. (2001) *Nurturing Emotional Literacy*, David Fulton, London.

Useful resources for further emotional literacy work

Rae, T. *Dealing with Feeling, An Emotional Literacy Curriculum*, Lucky Duck Publishing, Bristol.

Rae, T. and Robinson, G. *Keep your Coooool, Stress Reducing Strategies for Key Stage 2 & 3*, Lucky Duck Publishing, Bristol.

Face it, A deck of 52 cards which display 13 different expressions across a variety of age groups. Ten different games are given. Some are simple enough to use with key stage one children, other games are suitable for use with key stages two and three. Available though Smallwood Publishing, Tel: 01304 226900.

All about me, A useful communication game that helps pupils to talk about their feelings in a small group setting. Available through Smallwood Publishing on 01304 226900.

For further resources and information about emotional literacy in general visit the National Emotional Literacy Interest Group website at www.nelig.com

Visit www.luckyduck.co.uk to see their most recent publications on emotional matters and issues.

The Feelings Diary

Photocopiable sheets

There are many different types of photocopies in schools, from simple one page copiers to sophisticated machines that copy double sided and collate the pages. We have tried to provide copiable sheets that will suit all machines. Our key copies are double sided. They can be used whilst bound into the book or removed by neatly cutting along the dotted lines.

Covers

- ▶ Front and back cover
- ▶ Inside front and back cover

These are best copied onto coloured paper or card.

Diary sheets

To provide maximum flexibility and to allow the facilitator to produce as many weeks of the diary as suits the duration of the programme, the diary sheets are not specific to a day of the week.

We have provided the following diary model.

Monday	Tuesday	Wednesday	Thursday	Friday	Saturday	Sunday

- ▶ The pupils can colour/shade/tick the day of the week and/or inset the date
- ▶ Alternatively, the teacher could inset the appropriate dates before photocopying

Photocopy as many pages as necessary.

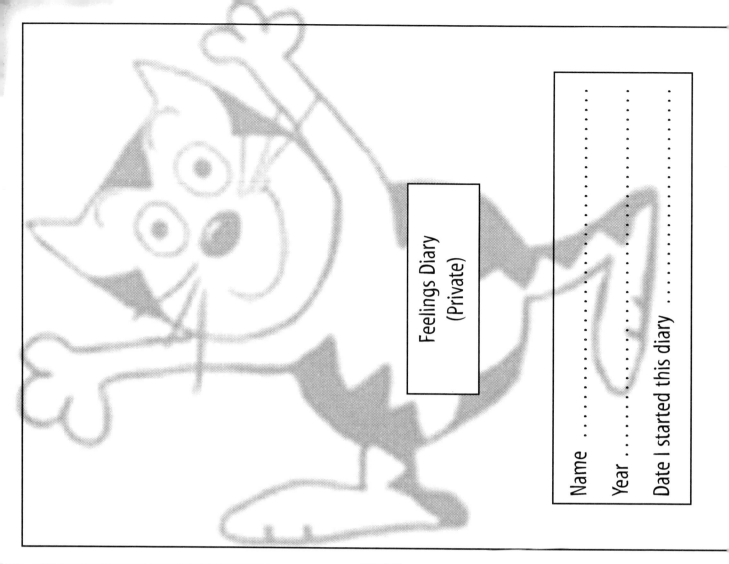

Feelings Diary
(Private)

Name ....

Year ....

Date I started this diary ....

You can help yourself feel better!

We all have uncomfortable feelings from time to time. For example, feeling lonely, sad, guilty, embarrassed or angry. You don't have to keep feeling that way though. Did you know that sometimes there are things you can do to help yourself feel better?

You've already gone some way to helping change your feelings by simply using this diary to sort out just what it is you are feeling.
Here are a few ideas of things you can do. I'm sure you can think of lots more that are even better for you personally.

▶ Talk to someone about how you are feeling and why

▶ Take some exercise, go for a walk or a run or play football

▶ Listen to some fun, upbeat music

▶ Do something you enjoy. Go to the cinema or go round to a friend's house for a chat. If you can't go out give them a ring (remember to get permission first)

▶ Think about how you want to feel right now, happy? relaxed? Picture how you would look and what you would be doing if you felt like that

▶ Do something nice for someone else. Buy them a bar of chocolate or help out with the housework. Give someone a really nice surprise

▶ Sometimes it's helpful just to accept uncomfortable feelings. Try saying to yourself, 'OK I feel really angry/sad/ lonely, right now, but this feeling will pass'

This is your personal diary where you can write or draw how you are feeling each day.

Aims

How do you want to feel each day?

Relaxed

Thankful

Happy

Calm

Proud

Monday | Tuesday | Wednesday | Thursday | Friday | Saturday | Sunday

How I felt today

Good Feelings

Relaxed · Surprised · Proud · Sad · Bored · Lonely · Angry

OK · Thankful · Excited · — · Frustrated · Tired

Peaceful · Happy · Giggly · Worried · Fed up · Scared

Uncomfortable Feelings

Why? Write or draw here. . .

Maybe you don't want to feel like you do. Turn to the back page for some ideas on how you can help yourself when you have uncomfortable feelings

---

Feelings Diary: Inside spread

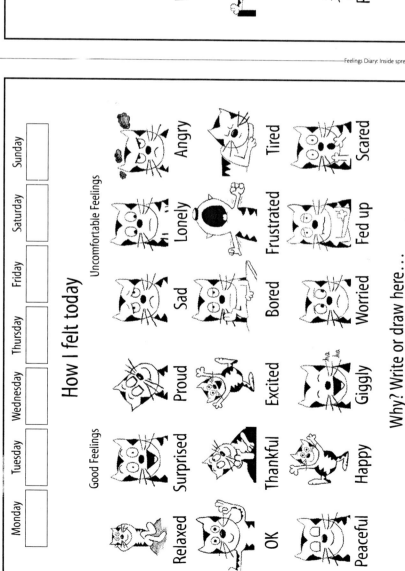

Monday | Tuesday | Wednesday | Thursday | Friday | Saturday | Sunday

How I felt today

Good Feelings

Relaxed · Surprised · Proud · Sad · Bored · Lonely · Angry

OK · Thankful · Excited · — · Frustrated · Tired

Peaceful · Happy · Giggly · Worried · Fed up · Scared

Uncomfortable Feelings

Why? Write or draw here. . .

Maybe you don't want to feel like you do. Turn to the back page for some ideas on how you can help yourself when you have uncomfortable feelings